GIVE IT UP!

GIVE IT UP!

A LENTEN STUDY FOR ADULTS

Dottie Escobedo-Frank

Abingdon Press
Nashville

Library of Congress Cataloging-in-Publication Data

Escobedo-Frank, Dottie.
  Give it up! : a lenten study for adults / Dottie Escobedo-Frank.
    pages cm
  ISBN 978-1-4267-8596-2 (trade pbk. : alk. paper) 1. Lent--Prayers and devotions. I. Title.
  BV85.E75 2014
  263'.92--dc23

                                       2014031978

14 15 16 17 18 19 20 21 22 23—10 9 8 7 6 5 4 3 2 1
MANUFACTURED IN THE UNITED STATES OF AMERICA

Contents

Give It Up!
A Journey of Release and Gain

We go through life applauding our heroes. We clap for sports heroes, for conference presenters, for the boss's yearly speech, and for our children at their school plays. And over time, we have developed a phrase that calls an audience to appreciative applause: "Give it up for . . ." Perhaps you can remember announcers of famous people saying something like, "Give it up for Beyonce!" Then a burst of thunderous applause raises the roof.

The most life-changing event in all of time is undoubtedly the moment when Jesus rose from the dead. If angels have wings, I'm sure they were flapping them in praise while singing a heavenly chorus. In fact, I can just imagine the whole universe joining them with an incredible light, color, and wind show. Surely, even the flowers put out their very strongest perfume for this moment of joy. If you and I were there when Jesus' body changed from *dead* to *alive*, we would probably *give it up* with applause, tears, jumps of joy, and shouts of amazement. But history records no human response of applause.

At Jesus' birth, there was the joy of the shepherds, the journey of the wise folk, and the adoration of Mama and

Daddy. But no one cried out to the town to "give it up for Jesus!" at his entry into our world.

We don't know what it was like to meet Jesus when he walked the earth. But we imagine what it might be like to meet him someday. The song "I Can Only Imagine" by Mercy Me touches on the moment in which we meet Jesus face-to-face at the end of our days on this earth. It asks:

Will I sing hallelujah, will I be able to speak at all?
I can only imagine

Last year, my parents both died and entered into eternity. I knew that would happen someday, but I didn't know that it would happen in January and June of 2013. We like to think death is always out in the future and not something we grapple with today. But as my brothers and sisters and I released our parents back to God, we had some very tough and some very holy moments. There was still leftover sadness and anger and all those phases of grief that eventually turn to acceptance and celebration of life, but knowing God would be with them comforted us in the end. Release was part of our healing, and it only happened because we knew that somehow, somewhere, God received them.

So we have spent time imagining what it would be like to enter into heaven, into the glory of God, but we haven't wrapped our minds around the moment that changed everything in the world: that moment when Jesus rose from the grave and came back to life on earth, before entering life in eternity again. It's the most incredible moment in history, yet when we think of it today, we don't stop to applaud or jump for joy or shout out loud. Instead, we put out a basket of candy for the kiddos and talk about a bunny and go to church with Mama—watered-down joy for the most amazing moment in all time.

So I was thinking about this in light of Lent, that season of the Christian year in which we remember the suffering Christ endured in the prelude to resurrection. That prelude was somber and sad and ended in death. That prelude to Easter is what we remember during Lent. We remember the suffering, the sorrow, and the lost hope.

So while it makes sense to "give it up" for Easter, it doesn't really make sense to applaud for Lent. It would be more appropriate to weep about the event that turned out the light of life (John 1:4), that shook the earth and tore the curtain of the Temple in two (Matthew 27:51). During Lent, we connect with those who responded to Jesus' death with tears and anguish. It doesn't feel like a time for applause.

I remember one time after my dad died when we were taking Mom to dinner across the street from the rehabilitation center. It was a pizza place, and we went there because it was close enough to roll Mom's wheelchair to and because the grandkids would like the pizza. Mom, though, was never a fan of pizza. But when we got in and started ordering, Mom suddenly started crying. We asked her why she was crying, and she explained that Dad always loved pizza, and smelling it made her miss him. We all surrounded Mom to comfort her, but the one who got there first was four-year-old Niko. He is a sensitive soul, and as soon as Mom teared up, Niko popped out of his chair and climbed onto my mother's lap. He stayed close to his great grandma throughout dinner, and he rode on her lap in the wheelchair afterward as we headed back to rehab. Niko knew instinctively that sometimes you just have to stay close when the tears fall.

We know how to *cry* with death, but we don't know how to *give it up* at death's stronghold.

I'm going to ask you to do something for Lent that will bring you significant joy in the end. And it will also bring you closer to the suffering of Jesus—not very close, for who can imagine what Jesus really went through—but suffering of a kind that matters in your life today.

This kind of suffering will include giving up something every week. And the intention is that as you release something, you gain something else. We don't always know how to release what has its hold on us or even that we need to release it, but when we let go of some part of our life that has a grip on us, we become open to new possibilities for living greatly. And for that, we certainly want to *give it up*!

I invite you to the journey of giving up something different each week. This will include

Week 1: mirrors
Week 2: social media
Week 3: talking
Week 4: TV and Internet stations
Week 5: cell phones
Week 6: all of the above

It's my hope that you can give up each of these things Monday through Saturday, leaving Sunday as a rest from your fast. If you are not able to commit to the full fast— giving up mirrors, for example—try it for three days or at the very least for one day. The longer you can experience each of these fasts, the deeper the learning will be. So try, if at all possible, to give up each item for six days of the week.

This journey requires some advance preparation, which will be explained each week. I would encourage you to write or talk about your experience to allow the learnings to be shared and documented. Learning new things takes effort, courage, and determination.

I pray that your experience of giving it up for Lent brings you to the place of *giving it up* for the moment that changed all our lives: Jesus' resurrection from death, the moment we call Easter.

Easter is not about the bunny or the Peeps candy or the ham-and-potato dinner with coconut cream pie. Easter is about breaking down the doors of hell and death and entering into the kingdom of heaven on earth.

I hope you jump and dance and weep and fall to your knees—because knowing how very much God loves you is reason to celebrate!

So let's all *give it up* for Jesus!

Dottie Escobedo-Frank

Mirror, Mirror . . .

Scripture: Read Philippians 4:8-9

GIVE IT UP: No mirrors for a week

GAIN: Internal significance

Every morning we roll out of bed, and before we face the world, we get a shower, put on our makeup or shave, fix our hair, and get dressed. Much of our little routine is performed in front of a mirror. We have mirrors in our bathrooms, our bedrooms, our entryways, our cars, our offices, and in our purses for emergency occasions. There is even an app for a mirror on our smartphones. Before we go to an interview or a meeting with a friend or even join a crowd, we often check our faces in the mirror to make sure there are no signs of leftover lunch or tiredness from too much work and not enough sleep. Mirrors are central in our experience of living in the modern day.

If you're not convinced, count the times you looked in a mirror today. My guess is you'll be surprised. Whether or not it's intentional, we check on ourselves as a confidence booster and out of habit.

According to *YouGov*, an online news source, we spend a significant amount of time getting ready every morning. Most of us (fifty-six percent) take eleven to thirty minutes. In addition, thirty-eight percent of women and twenty-one percent of men take longer than thirty minutes. That adds up to more than seven-and-a-half days every year working to look good.[1] And we spend high dollars on beautification as well. According to *Investopedia.com*, in 2008, Americans spent $7 billion on cosmetics, $1.5 billion on breast augmentation, $1 billion on tummy tucks, and $1.3 billion on liposuction. The average woman spends $1,000 per year on beauty products.[2] And while I, too, spend my fair share of time in front of the mirror trying to make myself look beautiful (or at least *better*) before I meet the world, I'm aware that the time could be better spent in other ways. I wonder what I could do with an extra week every year of my life.

The Scripture

The text in Philippians tells us that we could spend our time and effort on filling our minds and hearts with other things instead. We could, for example, think about truth and about what is noble. We could develop an authentic self that has a reputation to match. We could cultivate grace in our lives. Instead of focusing on the ugly, the cursed, and the worst of life, we could lean into what is beautiful, praiseworthy, and best.

The Philippian Christians were a small group who gathered to worship, possibly in the home of Lydia, a woman who traded in rich fabric (Acts 16:14). She was head of her household, providing well for her family. Paul wrote to the Philippians as he served time in a Roman prison, awaiting trial. He was well acquainted with the Christians in Philippi, and he wanted them to focus on what was going on inside their hearts and not on the outside. Some of them may have been cloth dealers like Lydia, handling costly fabrics for royalty. Some might have wished they could afford clothing made from the materials they dyed for others. So when Paul told them to focus inwardly, it was like telling a cosmopolitan model to get her picture taken for a national photo shoot but not to worry about what she looked like.

Was Paul doing the same thing? Was Paul trying to ignore his outward appearance? I wonder if Paul was thinking about how to strengthen his faith while he sat in a cold, stinking, and lonely jail. I wonder if his words to the Philippians were also to encourage *him* and to remind him that he still had hope for positive inward change even while he was helpless to change his outward situation. I wonder if he dealt with his chains by reminding himself that no one could shackle his thinking and that he could always choose freedom of mind and soul. His body may have been in chains, but there was more for Paul than his physical comfort.

Did you notice that the Scripture text asks us to work on the internal things? Not one item listed in the Scripture is an outward or visible object. And yet, in our world, we spend much time on our outward appearance, perhaps at the expense of inward attributes. What good can come of focusing on our insides while ignoring our outward appearance? Quite a bit, actually.

One Lenten Journey

I once spent all of Lent (forty days plus six Sundays) not looking in the mirror. I realized during the first day that I had to cover all my mirrors in my house with towels and sheets in order not to look inadvertently in the mirror. I counted the mirrors in my house and was astonished to find I had ten! I also had three mirrors in my car and two in my office. And almost everywhere I went in public, mirrors seemed to glare out at me.

My days changed significantly because of not looking in the mirror. In the morning, it took much less time to get ready. With no mirror to check my appearance in, I eliminated my usual routine of changing my outfit three or four times, and it took me only five minutes to put on the one I did choose. My makeup and hair routine changed as well. At first, I just put a little makeup on, hoping I wasn't smudging anything, but eventually I gave that up and went sans makeup. My hair routine underwent a similar change. I couldn't see how it looked, so over time I gave up caring. I went through the motions of brushing my hair, but I had no idea if the effort was worth it. My daughters were helpful; they would let me know if something was out of place or smudged, while still honoring my need to not really attend too closely to my looks.

At first, I found it hard not to view myself in a mirror. Without thinking, I would look several times a day, which is why I just ended up covering all mirrors at home and at work. I actually had to remind myself to stay away from mirrors at first. And of course, there are mirrors in our environment that can't be covered: your rearview mirror (I used that only for driving), the mirrors in restaurants, and glass-plated windows on the streets. Bathrooms almost always have mirrors, so I learned to look down while washing my hands. It was like playing a game of dodge ball, and there were one hundred places to dodge every day.

My clothing choices went through a transformation. I began to choose only what was comfortable. And realizing it is silly to dress without comfort, I added my uncomfortable clothes to the giveaway pile. Sometimes I asked my husband if I looked stupid in an outfit. He would say, "No!" which is what he always said; yet surprisingly, it made me feel better! I had to release myself from caring about my outward appearance, and it was a painful process.

I learned some things along the way, including what things I had to avoid in order not to use a mirror. They included

- *not* getting a haircut (can't avoid the salon mirror)
- *not* picking out a new pair of glasses
- *not* buying clothing
- *not* putting on most of my makeup
- *not* doing yoga (mirrors everywhere)

Mirror-less living puts some limits on life. Sometimes I would catch myself looking down to avoid the possibility of a mirror up ahead. The world seemed different; it was filled with that which I was trying to avoid!

Somewhere into the second week, I got comfortable without mirrors. And I even started noticing something akin to mirrors: *reflections*—reflections in the metallic spout of my kitchen faucet, in windows bathed in sunshine, on computer screens, in my coffee cup, and even in the chocolate brown eyes of my friend. I was dazzled by reflections even though I'd hardly noticed them before. But that says something about life: Our things are reflections of who we are, and our friends are reflections of ourselves. I suspect that when God asked us to take care of the earth and the people in it, it was because in caring for them, we would be working on the reflection of our own souls. I wonder if God made reflections to occur in so many places around us so that we would not forget how connected we are—that for better or for worse, we are similar to those around us and that we will never be left alone. Proverbs 27:19 says it well: "As water reflects the face, so the heart reflects one person to another."

The Internal Journey

What continued to rise up during that mirror-less time was the demand to be myself without outward distractions—to be real and true and to be comfortable in my own soul. I can't even begin to explain how good that feels. Sometimes we get distracted by our *outer* selves to the point of forgetting our *inner* selves.

The journey of an entire Lenten season without mirrors made me wish everyone could do this at least once. It especially made me wish that those who make a living on their looks could go forty days without mirrors. What would change if Madonna, the Kardashians, or Pink went without a mirror? Or what about people who care so much to fit in by their looks: CEOs of companies and heads of institutions? What if all pastors, bishops, and church attendees spent a Lenten season without mirrors? Would it change our church?

At the end of this journey, I realized I had gained so much. New freedoms popped up everywhere. I cared less about the exterior things of life because I didn't see them in relation to myself. "Seeing is believing" had a new meaning for me as I chose to see less of myself and more of the world around me. I didn't judge myself so harshly because I wasn't using the mirror as a weapon against myself or as a standard. I felt kindness well up within me toward myself, and I had an incredible sense of goodness inside. It's hard to explain except to say it really felt good to be comfortable in my skin again, much like I felt as a child.

I saw others more clearly and listened more deeply. I experienced the meaning of this Scripture differently: "Now we see a reflection in a mirror; then we will see face-to-face. Now I know partially, but then I will know completely in the same way that I have been completely known" (1 Corinthians 13:12).

On Easter morning, I broke my mirror fast. At first, I forgot to use the mirrors while getting dressed. Then I remembered and laughed because I really didn't need the mirror anymore. But I looked at the one thing I hoped to see again. I looked in the mirror and into my eyes. "Yep! I'm still here." I did miss seeing the reflection of my soul in my eyes. As Matthew 6:22 reminds us, the eyes are important because they are the light of the body. I did enjoy seeing that light.

I noticed that I was outwardly the same, but inwardly forever changed. It changed the meaning of that old saying, "Mirror, mirror on the wall, who's the fairest of them all?" Forty days without mirrors made me see the beauty in all of us. Thank God for the experiment of mirror-less living.

Questions for Reflection and Discussion

1. Do you remember the first time you saw yourself in a mirror? Or, have you ever seen a reflection of yourself that looked different than you expected? What did you think about yourself at that moment?

2. Who is the most beautiful person you know? Would he or she be able to fit the perception of a highly paid model in New York? Why do you see him or her as beautiful?

3. How many mirrors do you have in your home and your workplace? In what ways do you depend on them?

4. Do you think you are beautiful or good-looking? Do you think you are beautiful on the inside? Describe your unique beauty.

5. Think about someone who is beautiful but thinks she or he is ugly. What comes to your mind when that person puts herself or himself down?

6. Will it be easy for you to go without mirrors this week? Project how long you think you'll last.

Prayer

Dear God, you encompass every beam of light and every reflection. We have forgotten that we exist for love and joy and that we, too, are a reflection of you. Forgive us for judging ourselves too harshly and for judging others according to unreachable standards. Give us the grace to look into one another's eyes and to see you. We have changed ourselves because we have been ruled by our outward appearance. So help us change back to the beautiful and varied souls that are content with different earthly expressions of a heavenly state. Help us to love ourselves as we are so that we can love others more expressively. Guard our thoughts and emotions for your glory. Amen.

Focus for the Week

Try to go six days, Monday through Saturday, without a mirror. If you can't make it for six days, attempt to reach at least three days without looking at yourself in a mirror. Focus instead on the internal goodness in yourself and in others.

---

1. From "The Morning Routine: 30% spend over a week in getting ready each year," by Kate Palmer for *YouGov*, July 10, 2012. *https://today.yougov.com/news/2012/07/10/morning-routine-30-spend-over-week-getting-ready-e/*. Accessed March 8, 2014.

2. From "Cutting Personal Care Costs: It's a Beautiful Thing," by Amy Bell for *Investopedia*, October 16, 2009. *www.investopedia.com/financial-edge/1009/cutting-personal-care-costs-its-a-beautiful-thing.aspx*.

Social Butterfly

Scripture: Read Mark 12:28-31

GIVE IT UP: No social media for a week (except for business, work, and school e-mails)

GAIN: Socialization in real time

The phrase *social butterfly* refers to someone "who is social or friendly with everyone, flitting from person to person, the way a butterfly might."[1] We use this phrase when we see someone who talks to many people at a party, enjoys gathering social connections, and has many friends in different aspects of life. Social butterflies are at ease in large groups, love going to parties or watching sports at a sports bar, and are not bothered by walking into a meeting or class that has already started without them. They have confidence in handling almost all social situations. They are usually friendly, agreeable, and easygoing. They have deep confidence in their social space.

My husband is a social butterfly. No matter where we are, he recognizes people, can recall where he met them, and can tell you a little about their story. The breadth of his connections amazes me. While I am hesitant to go to parties, he can't wait to be fully engaged at an event. He is a connector, introducing people to others because they might benefit from meeting each other. He remembers names without having to use mnemonic name games.

However, in the world of social media, *social butterfly* might take on a new meaning. It could refer to someone who has the most followers or tweets on Twitter, the most friends on Facebook, or the most pins shared on Pinterest. In the social media world, even an introvert can be popular and well-known. Posting and responding to social media, frankly, requires alone time. So with social media, one can be both reclusive and a social butterfly.

This week, I'm asking you to give up social media for six days (except as necessary for work or family emergencies). You may think this will be easy, and perhaps it will be. But through the challenge of going without social media, you will find out whether or not it is a huge part of your life.

Social Media Front-and-Center

Arianna Huffington, in her book *Thrive: The Third Metric to Redefining Success and Creating a Life of Well-Being, Wisdom, and Wonder* includes a section titled, "Overconnectivity: The Snake in Our Digital Garden of Eden." She reminds us that most smartphone users check their phone every six-and-a-half minutes, which adds up to about 150 times per day. And the most difficult aspect of our overuse of smartphones is that "there is evidence that it can begin to actually rewire our brains to make us less adept at real human connection."[2]

According to a recent report in *Medical News Today*, the use of Facebook may be causing an increase in anxiety and feelings of inadequacy. The report includes several comments and assertions. Ethan Cross, a social psychiatrist at the University of Michigan, stated the irony of connection via social media: "On the surface, Facebook provides an invaluable resource for fulfilling the basic human need for social connection. But rather than enhance well-being, we found that Facebook use predicts the opposite result—it undermines it."[3]

While Facebook's mission is to help us connect with others, our overuse is causing a disconnect in real-time relationships. And for this, we are suffering bouts of isolation and loneliness. Using Facebook to connect with friends is so prevalent that a test has been developed to measure Facebook addiction; it's called the Bergen Facebook Addiction Scale (BFAS).[4] This suggests a need for us to establish boundaries on our usage so that social media can be a tool and not a demon.

Nonetheless, there are apparently some positive effects as well. For example, social media may be providing us with a way to deal with life's pain and difficulties. Dr. Shannon M. Rauch, from the Benedictine University in Mesa, Arizona, states that we use social media for relief of boredom and for distraction from the self. A study from the University of California at San Diego, which is included in the *Medical News Today* report, connects social media use with the spread of general happiness,[5] which seems to contradict Ethan Cross's statement above. Maybe it's too soon to be sure either way. But it's likely that we receive both benefits and detriments from our social media usage.

So why does it matter whether or not we are connected to social media 24-7? The truth is we can benefit greatly if we control the tool instead of having the tool control us. But sometimes, to determine how controlled we are by social media, we have to take a timeout and see what happens in our lives when social media is no longer front-and-center.

The Scripture

In Mark 12:28-31, one of the religious scholars, who has heard Jesus' previous brilliant responses to questions, asks him a critical one: Which of the Law's commandments is the most important? Jesus answers with a combination command. First, quoting from Deuteronomy 6:4-5: "Israel, listen! Our God is the one Lord, and you must love the Lord your God with all your heart, with all your being, with all your mind, and with all your strength." And second, from Leviticus 19:18: "You will love your neighbor as yourself." And Jesus adds, "No other commandment is greater than these."

In effect, Jesus condenses all of the commandments down to two so that we can understand what matters in life and so that we can know how to sift through the choices that come to us. Jesus, you could say, makes it very plain!

If you wanted to make these commandments even simpler, you could say, "Listen and love!"

So it's simple: Listen and love God, and listen to and love our neighbors. Listening and loving sound like things we can all live with and make happen in our lives. Listening requires attention, presence, and interest. And listening to our neighbors happens best when we are present enough to read body language as well as hear the words. Perhaps you have had the experience of communicating poorly in an e-mail and later clearing up the misunderstanding quickly with a face-to-face conversation. Many miscommunications could be prevented if we talked with each other in person instead of via e-mail.

And loving seems normal enough. We love what and who are easy to love: our friends, our family, our political views, our animals, our form of art. Loving is part of our natural life. But sometimes we don't love with the depth and tenacity that real love requires. It's harder to love our enemies, some of our family members, people with a different political view from ours, and those who express themselves with alternative forms of art. Have you ever caught yourself judging someone because of his or her tattoos or loud music? That is their form of art, yet we have trouble loving what we don't understand. Loving is both natural and unnatural, depending on the circumstances.

So Jesus asks us to listen and love. But we can't listen and love well if we are connected constantly to social media. We lose touch with those closest to us when we turn on the computer or use our phones to text the person sitting in the room with us to get their attention. Loving involves listening without the distraction that social media brings. Perhaps, in this day, social media is our biggest distraction from really loving our neighbor and our self. Maybe it's more distracting than other addictions, even if seemingly more innocent. It can be more distracting than romance or joy. Maybe the distraction of social media is so entwined in our lives that it is indistinguishable from life itself. We will only know if we try to take it away for a week or a day.

Life Without Social Media

The week I chose to live without social media (taking note only of work-related e-mails), I was attending a retreat for pastors. It helped that Wi-Fi wasn't available in my room, and it helped that much of our time was taken up in workshops. I found myself wanting to check my e-mails regularly but limited the times that I actually did so. Because of that, I was able to have more conversations with people in real time. I heard stories of their lives and pains and joys that I might not have heard if I had rushed off to my room to check on my work. It was hardest to stay off Twitter, Facebook, and Pinterest, and I found that social media occupies much of my thoughts and time. I came away from that retreat wanting to find a method to limit the time I give to electronic communication so that I could spend more time in face-to-face communication.

There are many ways to guard our relationships and our time from the impact of too much social media. We can check our phone at the door—or at the docking station—when we enter our homes, and refuse to carry them from room to room. We can establish rules about when we can use social media and when it is impolite or improper. Perhaps at dinner or at bedtime we can release ourselves from the connection with those outside our habitats. We can limit the number of times we check social media, perhaps to three times per day. Or we might decide to attend to social media for one hour per day, and make it a time that doesn't affect the rest of our day (say 4–5 P.M. when most of our work is completed). These are just ideas to get you thinking about limiting your access to social media for a week.

I would like to challenge you to release yourself fully from social media just for six days, insofar as it is possible. That will help you understand how much you rely on it. Take note of how often you think you'd like to post something or check a post. Recall how often you unthinkingly reach for your smartphone as a habit. Check out how much time you have to talk to people in your personal space and whether or not you have anything to say.

Use this time to listen well. Use this time to love well. That is what Jesus requires of us.

So for one week, we won't be distracted from listening or loving by the presence of our social media tools. We will put our tools in the back seat for a while and put each other and God in the front seat again. There will be some agony and some discomfort—and some light-bulb moments. And my hope is that you gain socialization in real time—and therein learn to listen and love again.

Questions for Reflection and Discussion

1. Do you think you might be addicted to social media? How often do you reach for your phone to text, check e-mails or Facebook, and so forth per day?

2. Is there someone you love who, in your opinion, is overly connected to social media? How does it affect your relationship with that person?

3. Who is the youngest person you know who accesses social media? What is that person's age? How did she or he learn to use social media?

4. When is the last time you attended a small gathering and left your phone behind? Do you feel uncomfortable without your phone nearby?

5. Can you describe the times you feel most heard?

6. How can you listen and connect better with people this week? What do you hope to gain by fasting from social media?

Prayer

God of Life, you encouraged us to love you and others and ourselves well, yet we have fallen short of this calling. We have let things and tools and habits intrude on our ability to love well. Forgive us. Set us free from our addiction to the tools so that we can become the loving community you call us to be. Set us free from the addictions we don't recognize or won't admit to. Set us free to spill our love into your world. Show us how to connect deeply with those we love and those who are lonely and lost without us. Remind us of your love that surpasses everything we can understand. Thank you for helping us grow. Amen.

Focus for the Week

Give up social media for six days. This means no e-mails, texts, or social sites (except those necessary for work). Use your phone for voice conversations only. If you can't do it for all six days, try it for three or four days. Or if you must, limit social media to one hour per day. The gain is socialization in real time, which produces love in real time as well.

1. From *www.vocabulary.com/dictionary/social*.
2. From *Thrive: The Third Metric to Redefining Success and Creating a Life of Well-Being, Wisdom, and Wonder*, by Arianna Huffington (Harmony Books, 2014); page 62.
3. From "Social media: How does it really affect our mental health and well-being?" in *Medical News Today*, April 16, 2014. *www.medicalnewstoday.com/articles/275361.php*. Accessed May 6, 2014.
4. From "Facebook Addiction—New Psychological Scale," in *Medical News Today*, May 11, 2012. *www.medicalnewstoday.com/articles/245251.php*.
5. From "Social media: How does it really affect our mental health and well-being?"

Talk, Talk, Talk!

Scripture: Read 1 Kings 19:9-18

GIVE IT UP: No talking for a week (except as absolutely needed for work, school, or family)

GAIN: Listening deeply to God and people and the sounds of life

The Scripture

Elijah was hiding out for his life. He'd made the wrong woman mad. Queen Jezebel was furious that her prophets of Baal had died, and Elijah was to blame (see 1 Kings 18:20-40; 19:1-2). So she put him on a hit list. Elijah, badly frightened, ran to the desert and collapsed in the shade of a bush, wishing only to die. (I grew up in the desert, and I can tell you that the shade of a desert bush is not very protective in the heat of the day!) He was petrified, sick of politics, feeling put upon, and exhausted (1 Kings 19:4-5). But God saw him in this place of hiding, and sent an angel to wake him up and feed him bread and water. After he ate, he slept (verses 5-6). After one more round of eating, he set out and walked for forty days and nights until he came to

Mount Horeb, the mountain of God. Elijah was running for his life and hoping to find God on the sacred mountain. (Sometimes when everything is going wrong in our lives, we too need to take forty days to go to seek after God. Or take a hike on a mountain, and see if God meets us there.) When Elijah arrived, he found a cave where he spent the night (1 Kings 19:8-9).

Finally, after the long hike in the desert, after exhaustion and rest, after agony and much defeatist thinking, Elijah heard God ask, "Why are you here, Elijah?" (verse 9). That's a funny question because, of course, God knows what's up with Elijah. God has been following him around, feeding him and making sure he has water on his long, dry trek. But God wanted Elijah to open up to God, so God questions him with the obvious: "Why are you here?"

Elijah tells God his story. He says he has spent his life working hard for God and that he is so discouraged because the people have deserted God's way. Not only that, but the worship centers are destroyed and the prophets have been killed. And now, they are out to kill me too, the weary prophet says. You can almost hear the anguish in his voice and the exhaustion of living a life for God that turned out to be very hard (verses 10-11).

So God tells Elijah to stand up and pay attention, and God will show up for him, for his life and for his troubles.

Elijah stands up and notices a hurricane—a "strong wind"—that crumbles the rocks. But he doesn't experience God in the wind.

Elijah then feels the tremble and movement of an earthquake. But the prophet doesn't find God in the earthquake. Then Elijah sees a devastating fire. But God isn't in the fire. Finally, after the hurricane, the earthquake, and the fire, Elijah hears a quiet whisper. The New Revised Standard Version of the Bible says that Elijah hears, "a sound of sheer silence." When he hears that sound, he covers his face in fear, because he recognizes that God is in the whisper. And in that whisper God asks again, "Why are you here, Elijah?" (verse 13).

Elijah knows that God hears him and that God is present, and he tells God again that things have gone so wrong in his life. He explains that he works hard for God; but despite his work, God's people have abandoned God's covenant, the houses of worship are destroyed, and the prophets of God have been killed. Then Elijah adds, "I'm the only one left, and now they want to take my life too" (verse 14).

Can you hear Elijah's desperation and loneliness? Have you ever been in the place where you felt all alone and desperate for your life? Perhaps you've called out to God, just hoping God was listening. Or maybe you heard God's whisper and you knew God was paying attention, so you called out hoping God would change what you could not.

God spoke to Elijah and told him to go back and do God's bidding. Elijah was to anoint a new king and also to anoint Elisha as his successor. And God reminded the prophet that he was not alone and that seven thousand people were still devoted to God and God alone. God showed him that even in the middle of his terrible situation, there was something he could do and that things weren't as bleak as he thought. God showed him that God listened and was present to him.

Talk, Talk, Talk . . .

When I read Elijah's story, I was aware that it contained a litany of complaints. You can hear Elijah "talk, talk, talk" to God and to himself, repeating details of his terrible situation over and over in his head. And sometimes we do the same. We pray our list of "terribles" repeatedly:

> *O God, please take away this terrible boss who hates me. O God, please fix my ungrateful family. O God, please change my terrible, unbearable life . . .*

We look at the places in our lives where the earth has shaken, where the winds have destroyed, and where the fire has burned us out. We look at the areas of our life where the "sky is falling," and we fixate on those difficulties. We notice the loud crashes and destructions, and we talk, talk, talk our terribles to God. We hope God can fix us. But we don't take time to stop talking our complaints long enough to listen for the whisper of God's instructions.

A University of Arizona study in 2007 reported that, contrary to the popular notion that women talk more, men and women speak the same amount of words: sixteen thousand words per day.[1] That adds up to one hundred twelve thousand words every week. That's a lot of words! The Scriptures have some things to say to us about our excessive talking:

- "Don't be quick with your mouth or say anything hastily before God, because God is in heaven, but you are on earth. Therefore, let your words be few" (Ecclesiastes 5:2).
- "People who watch their mouths guard their lives, but those who open their lips are ruined" (Proverbs 13:3).

- "Set a guard over my mouth, Lord; keep close watch over the door that is my lips" (Psalm 141:3).

We need to use our words sparingly and carefully and exercise them wisely. Do you use your words to comfort and soothe or to bring about turmoil and agitation? Do your words speak of things that matter or are they a trivial flow of the mundane? Do your words cause people to sit up and listen, or to say, "Oh, he or she is just talking again!"

And one more question: What is the most frequent topic of your words? Sometimes, to understand the value of words, we need to take a break from talking so much, and lean into listening again.

When Presence Matters More

While we need to use our words for encouraging and loving others, there are times when we have no words to say. Life can take us to the point where we are speechless and don't know what to say in the face of extreme pain.

When my husband and I brought home our baby whose birth defect allowed us just a few days with her, our family and friends surrounded us. They didn't know what to say, but they came anyway. Some tried to say something comforting, but it usually came out bumbling and awkward. The wise ones just came near and brought a long hug, or food, or took the time to sit with us and hold our hands. Our families stayed through all the short days of our daughter's life, just to be near to us.

Elizabeth lived only four days, so each day was precious. One night, two of our friends from Houston, Monte and

Wayne, caught a plane and arrived at our house at midnight, and then took a plane back at 6 A.M. that same morning. They arrived and didn't have anything to say, but their presence spoke volumes of love. We called them our "midnight visitors," and we will never forget the love they expressed without saying a word.

Sometimes presence matters more than words. When you are present with someone, you set aside your own needs, and you open up to the need of the other. When we are present, we hear others through their own experiences and not through the filter of our own understandings. When we are present, we are a gift that ushers in God's love to another.

The Healthy Silence

An old adage states, "It is better to be silent and be thought a fool, than to speak and remove all doubt." But while this saying is worthy of note, there is a deeper reason for silence than not wanting to look the fool. Silence brings value to our lives in ways not always noted:

- Creativity is enhanced with silence. Artists know that an imposed silence can encourage the creative spirit. Twyla Tharp, in her book *The Creative Habit: Learn It and Use It for Life*, says that silence is "the perfect editor for the creative soul."[2]
- Silence is good therapy. Ask monks and religious leaders who take silent retreats.
- Silence increases focus. Remember what it is like to have to study and how silence increases your ability to recall and focus on the subject matter at hand.

- Silence makes you more thoughtful. We are able to hear our souls speak through silence. Roberta Matuson writes, "It's often the quiet ones who out-produce everyone else."[3]
- Silence increases listening skills.[4]

Culture also has an effect on our ability to learn value from silence. In *Quiet: The Power Of Introverts in a World That Can't Stop Talking*, Susan Cain states, "In the West, we subscribe to the Extrovert Ideal, while in much of Asia (at least before the Westernization of the past several decades), silence is golden."[5] We in the West can learn from the quiet cultures and find ways to bring silence to the center of our work and life. Tibetan Buddhist monks, for example, score off the charts on happiness as they quietly meditate on compassion.[6] What values of health, creativity and productivity would we bring into our lives if we regularly established moments of silent retreat?

When we first visited England, our family rode trains from town to town. We encountered a quietness and stillness on the trains that was different from riding on public transportation in America. It was so noticeable that we took to whispering to one another, which seemed to fit the norm. One day while boarding a train, we noticed a car that had a sign on it: "Quiet Car." I asked someone what that meant. We were told that car was for people who wanted to work or read or be still without distracting noise. So no one talked on their cell phones or talked to each other if they chose to ride that car. I was surprised by the depth of the need to be quiet, a need that sometimes, in some cultures, even results in public spaces for quietness.

We can sometimes get in a rut of not paying attention and not hearing those close to us. When my daughter Natalie was about three years old, she was a great talker. She loved to share with us what she was thinking and often gave us input on how we could manage family situations better. I loved to hear Natalie talk for she had insight, understanding, and love way beyond her years. I remember once when she was talking, and I wasn't paying attention. She reached her little hands over to my face, and put one hand on each cheek. She turned my face to her so that I was looking right into her eyes, and she said, "Mama, you're not hearing me!" She wanted and called for my full attention. She wanted the look-me-in-my-eyes-when-I'm-talking kind of commitment. I delivered with my full self, listening with an inward chuckle. We all need to be heard as much as we need to listen.

A Week Without Talking

I'm asking you to take the next six days (Monday through Saturday) without talking. Of course, you should feel free to talk at work or school when appropriate, but find a way to keep silent at all other times. Prepare your friends and family for this upcoming week by letting them know you are fasting from the spoken word. Try to make it six days; but if that doesn't work for you, at least go one day without talking, or perhaps you could make it three days.

You will find it changes your life. A few years ago, I went a week without talking (except when necessary at work). I found the most difficulty when I was out in the public. When people said, "Hello!" for example, I naturally wanted to say hello in return. I found myself going out in public less and less as the week progressed. It was just too hard.

I also found out that I heard so many things that I hadn't heard before. I heard birds singing in the morning; I heard the tones of my husband's voice; I heard background music. The scope of my hearing increased, and the world came alive in a new way.

And as I found myself listening more, I was able to listen for God's voice as well. God speaks in the silence, in the whisper, in the stillness. We need to be poised to hear, and refusing to talk for a time helps us listen better.

This is the exciting part: We gain the ability to really hear others and to really hear God! It is worth the effort because what we hear can be surprising and refreshing.

Elijah heard God in a whisper. Whispering directions, God told the prophet how to get out of his messy situation.

This week I pray God speaks to you . . . in a whisper.

Questions for Reflection and Discussion

1. Who is the biggest talker in your family? How does that affect your family dynamic?

2. Do you talk more or listen more? Are you the center of attention at a party, or are you listening to others in social gatherings? In one-on-one settings, do you talk more or listen more?

3. Do you gain energy by being in a crowd and talking with others or by being quiet and having space for reflection?

4. When was the last time you heard God? What was that experience like for you? Describe your ability to hear God in that moment.

5. To whom do you most often listen for counsel or guidance? Does that person listen well?

6. Who taught you how to be a good listener?

Prayer

Dear God, we are reluctant to be still and hear you in a whisper. We cry out continually to hear your voice, yet we forget to stop talking and start listening. This week, help us to stop talking long enough to start hearing. Open our ears to hear things we haven't heard in a long time. Help us to hear our loved ones, our coworkers, and even our pets. Especially help us to hear you. Forgive us for our loud-talking ways, and bring us to the peace that comes from hearing you. Amen.

Focus for the Week

Give up talking for one week. If you must, talk at work or in important family situations, but be aware of talking too much. Lean into listening and make space for others to speak. Hear their words and their emotions, and feel their struggles as you set yourself aside and enter into another's world. Journal your thoughts as you give up talking.

1. From "Study: Women Don't Talk More Than Men," by Ashley Phillips for *ABC News, at abcnews.go.com/ Technology/story?id=3348076*. Accessed March 22, 2014.

2. From *The Creative Habit: Learn It and Use It for Life*, by Twyla Tharp (Simon & Schuster, 2003); page 32

3. From "The Link Between Quietness and Productivity," by Roberta Matuson for *Fast Company*, August 7, 2012. *http://www.fastcompany.com/3000226/link-between-quietness-and-productivity*.

4. From "The One Thing You're Not Doing That Will Completely Boost Your Focus," by Kate Bratskeir for *The Huffington Post*, August 28, 2013. *www.huffingtonpost.com/2013/08/28/benefits-of-quiet_n_3757687.html*. Accessed March 22, 2014.

5. From *Quiet: The Power of Introverts in a World That Can't Stop Talking*, by Susan Cain (Crown Publishers, 2012); page 190.

6. From *Quiet: The Power of Introverts in a World That Can't Stop Talking*; page 190.

Entertainment by Tube

Scripture: Read Isaiah 40:27-31

GIVE IT UP: No TV or Internet movie stations for a week

GAIN: Attention to cycles of rest and restoration time

When my children were little, they used to say they were "boy-trapped" or "girl-trapped" if they were surrounded by children of the opposite sex. I loved the phrase for its originality and descriptive qualities. I'd laugh outright at their tales of being surrounded by boys or girls! They were able to express succinctly that uncomfortable feeling of being out of their element.

Today, I would say that most of us are "screen-trapped." We grew up on television, rushing home from school to catch our favorite comedy. Some families began eating meals in front of a certain show or spending their evening after dinner watching a movie while eating popcorn. Going to the movies, with its big screen, became a popular date-night activity, fed by Hollywood's ideal of life. As time went by, we became further entrapped when we carried our laptop computers everywhere, and when we began to put screens on our phones. Now, with these screens, we can be at work 24-7 by checking e-mails and texting our coworkers. We can listen to music videos; we can peruse the Internet; and we can watch movies, all on our tiny screens. Education has joined the game with Internet readers, where we can download our books on an iPad, pay less for our books, and reduce the weight in our backpacks.

What's more, we often look at more than one screen simultaneously. I've been guilty of being on a computer working on a sermon, with my iPad open to a social media page, and my phone nearby in case I get a call. Now that is screen-trapped!

As I look at our lives surrounded by screens, I wonder if all this time on the screen is changing us, or at the very least, draining our energy.

The Scripture

Maybe the Israelites the prophet addressed in our Scripture reading had a similar problem. We all tend to whine and complain about our lives, and Israel (also called "Jacob" in the text) was no different. I would say they had a good reason to complain. They were in exile and wondered if God had forgotten about them. Life in captivity was difficult as Babylon continued to act as "power-over" them and even made it hard for them to practice their sacred religious ceremonies. They were just plain tired, and their energy was depleted. They had been beaten down in many areas of their lives. They were not just bone-tired and muscle-weak; they were soul-weary.

But the God who creates the vast earth is the same God who can intervene in human politics and societies. This God, the Scripture reminds us, does not get exhausted; and this God will provide Israel with strength and rest when its people are feeling weak and weary. God meets their plight with good news: You will receive restoration! It's like God is saying, "Hang on. Help is on the way! I've got this!" Salvation is running toward them.

We forget that sometimes. We forget God's promises to deliver us who trust God when there is nothing left inside. When we who trust God are weak, God promises energy for the whole walk of life—energy for the long run.

Maybe you can recall a time when your energy was drained and when you felt you had nothing left to go on. Maybe you had a moment when even the thought of getting a shower felt like too much work. You just wanted to lie in bed and pray that your strength would return. Getting moving and motivated seemed beyond your ability. And you certainly could not imagine walking briskly with a bounce in your step or running with lightness as in a Nike commercial. This Scripture meets us at points like this and gives us the good word of hope.

God goes into detail for the people addressed in this chapter of Isaiah. Speaking through the prophet, God reminds them that they have paid enough for their sins, and that now is their time to be comforted. God acknowledges their previous wrongdoing but then says, in effect, "We're done with that! Time to move on." The prophet then reminds the people who are suffering from lack of faith and limited strength that God's power is sufficient. God is "the creator of the ends of the earth" who "doesn't grow tired or weary" (verse 28).

Whenever God reminds us of the role of our Creator and the magnificence of the universe, we are put in our place, which is one of humility. But more than that, it is one of awe. We are in jaw-dropping, breath-inhaling, wide-eyed wonder when we look at creation and the Creator who brought it all to pass. How did God make the earth and the stars and the delicate skin of the flowers? How did God make the brown desert bloom yellow and the green meadows blossom emerald? How did God create the pesky, fire-burning ants and the softness of a kitten's fur? When we are reminded of God as Creator, we can set our anxiety down and know that God's power and awesomeness is beyond anything we will ever know.

For the Israelite captives, God's power is so amazing that they stop complaining and whining. God is about to bring them to a place of rest and restoration. God is about to answer their cries for help and hope, and they will be shocked by the depth of assistance God brings.

And so God promises energy to those who are tired, fresh strength to those who have dropped out, and strength to even the youth who have become exhausted. God promises that when they wait on God, they will receive the strength that is like the eagles who soar high above the earth, strength to run without getting tired, strength to walk without falling behind. This is God's promise to the people who have cried out in their time of pain.

Do You Need a Little Rest or Restoration?

We all have times when we can identify with the exiles' cry-out for strength and relief. Those in my profession are not known for being good at resting. In his book *Rest in the Storm: Self-Care Strategies for Clergy and Other Caregivers*, Kirk Byron Jones writes, "Clergy members must learn to confess personal overload and hurry as threats to our bodies (self and family), to the body of Christ, and to the body politic. We must confess insufficient self-care as a subtle but lethal expression of personal and social violence."[1]

Clergy are notorious for taking care of everyone at the expense of their own health. We laugh aloud when someone thinks that we only work on Sundays, because we know we rarely take a day off. Sometimes we announce proudly that we haven't had a day off in weeks, when really, a better position would be public repentance. Not to take care of ourselves is dangerous to our own lives, to the health of our families, and to our world.

Jones describes how, many years ago while pastoring a church in Pennsylvania, he found himself at the end of his rope—exhausted, stretched too thin, and weary. He was so busy fulfilling various roles—pastor, student, preacher, father, husband, and mentor—that he was neglecting the core of who he was. As he describes it, there was an underlying "me" calling out for rest and restoration, and he consistently ignored this inner voice. He eventually experienced a moment when it all caught up with him: "That me who had been ignored and suppressed for so long suddenly cried, 'No more!' while I was preaching in West Chester one night. Midway through the sermon, I turned to my seminary friend, Earl Trent, then pastor of St. Paul's Church, and said tersely, 'I can't go on!' I had come to my limit. I felt no physical pain, just a deep sense of fatigue that told me I could not go on."[2]

Jones walked off the pulpit in the middle of his sermon and sought treatment. He went to his doctor, who told him that physically he was fine. But the doctor asked him an important question: "What do you do to relax?"

Jones says that question changed his life. He couldn't think of one thing he did for fun. He listened as the doctor described how we all need rest and relaxation and how without it our bodies and souls become drained.[3]

Have you ever come to the end of your rope and wondered how you would have enough energy for the next moment? Are you there today? Are you weary and tired and worn out?

I love the fact that the titles of Jones' books show his attention to the change he made in his life:

- *Rest in the Storm: Self-Care Strategies for Clergy and Other Caregivers* (Judson Press, 2001)
- *Addicted to Hurry: Spiritual Strategies for Slowing Down* (Judson Press, 2003)
- *Fulfilled: Living and Leading with Unusual Wisdom, Peace, and Joy* (Abingdon Press, 2013)

Recognizing our emptiness is half the battle. Sometimes we just have to cry out to God for help in our time of weariness, like we hear in the song "Precious Lord, Take My Hand":

I am tired, I am weak, I am worn;
Take my hand, precious Lord, lead me home.[4]

God promises to take our hand and to lead us to the place of rest when weariness overtakes us. Our part is to stop the madness of "hurry" and ask God to restore us.

I Can Relate

I understand the kind of weariness Jones described and the exiles experienced. My weariness happened after too many meetings, too much fighting, and too little time away. It came slowly during a time when I was initially really energized about ministry. But gradually, I realized that my life source was being drained and that I needed to get away from ministry for a while. I felt so weary that I wanted just to go to a place where no one knew me and no one would talk to me.

So I begged my district superintendent for a renewal leave (and had to wait a year and a half to get it!). While waiting for a leave, I began intense self-care, recognizing that I could be in trouble if I didn't attend to my needs immediately. I made time every day to be alone, to study God's Word, and to consciously receive God's love. I read more than ever. I pulled away from unnecessary meetings. I gave in to the idea that God was in control of the outcome of ministry and that I was not.

When I was finally granted a month away (combined with two weeks of vacation), I headed to the beach in San Diego, rented a small apartment, and rested. Every day I woke up, walked on the beach, ate, slept, read, ate, watched the sunset, and went to bed. And then I did it again. And again. And again. The habit of rest was monotonous and wonderful at the same time.

The sound of the ocean has always felt like the breath of God to me, and so I inhaled God's breath daily. The in-and-out sound of the water hitting the sand gave me the message that God was breathing for the universe—and God was breathing with me. When you need rest, it's important to find the part of nature that ministers to you and spend time there. I missed my family eventually; but for a while, I just basked in the solitude, knowing that having nothing to do was good for my soul and necessary for my livelihood.

Six weeks came and went too quickly, and really, I could have stayed gone for a full three months; but it was enough to restore me to a place of health and wholeness. The interesting thing is that we often fight the urge to get away, thinking that our role is crucial to the lives of others, thinking the church (or work or the family) can't go on without us, thinking that we are indispensable. But the truth is that God has been running the world without our help for a very long time!

Sometimes God just wants us to respond to Jesus' invitation: "Come to me, all you who are struggling hard and carrying heavy loads, and I will give you rest" (Matthew 11:28).

Jesus invites us to come into his presence. Imagine what that might be like. Imagine that God holds you, takes the load off your shoulders, and sings you a sweet lullaby as you fall into a deeply restorative sleep: "Hush, little baby, don't you cry; Mama's gonna sing you a lullaby. . . ."[5]

Turning Off the Tube Provides Space to Rest

Perhaps one of the reasons we don't get enough rest is because our brains are always tuned in to our screens. When this happens, we don't have time to listen to the sound of God's breath or to feel the beauty of the night sky healing our broken souls. Maybe, if we gave ourselves a little more space every day, we could experience God's love more deeply.

So this week, for six days, we are going to turn off the screens: TV and any Internet station where we watch movies or shows.

We are going to slow down our in-home entertainment and discover how that changes our lives. The experiment is to see if on-screen entertainment occupies more time and space than we've realized and to figure out if spending less time in front of screens provides us with a sense of restoration.

The fact is we do spend a great portion of our lives in front of screens. According to a 2012 *New York Daily News* survey, children watch about 24 hours of TV a week, which translates to 3.5 hours per day (and equals 1,248 hours a year). It decreases slightly when we are teens, but then increases as we age, until people older than 65 years end up watching 48 hours a week (which is 7 hours a day).[6] That's a lot of life in front of a television.

Those numbers are just about television, but we know that today we can watch movies and shows on our computers via Netflix, Hulu, and so fourth and that we can access the tube anytime from our smartphones, tablets, and e-readers. For this reason, the statistics about TV watching might be lower than reality. We live a life now where we can be entertained by screens all hours of the day and night.

We use televisions and screens as loneliness-inhibitors, babysitters, and distractions from problems. We allow these devices to keep us from really living life with those in our homes, workplaces, and neighborhoods. We choose to live life via someone else's story on the screen. While TV can be a great source of relaxation, when it is used to excess, it can siphon energy away from living real life.

Many people consider viewing on-screen content as restful, and I agree . . . to a point. The problem is that we have become excessive with our televisions and screens, and our brains are constantly turned on and tuned in to someone else's anxiety.

We unknowingly participate in love triangles, murders, car chases, shootings, and crime scenes when we watch TV. That's exhausting, adrenaline-producing, and stress-maximizing. And it means we get very little downtime to release our own worry and very little time for resting without input. We were not created to live anyone else's life; we were made to live our own.

If you think about it, allowing our imaginations, emotions, and thought processes to be engaged through watching television and movies is like being on warp speed. It provides us little time to breathe through our own imaginations, emotions, and thoughts. The "other" takes up space in our lives, and we forget to live in the life that is ours. We make no space for restoring and breathing and feeling joy.

A Week Without Television or Internet Entertainment Channels

So I invite you to go six days without TV or movies or shows on the Internet. This means no movies, shows, or television news from Monday through Saturday. If your life at home revolves around the living room where the TV is the center of focus, you might have to find another room to use. If you can't talk to your spouse or children without the TV blaring, you might find that you hear better when the only sound in the room is their voices. You might even find that you miss TV so much that you are going through withdrawal. All these things will be signs to you of where your life is.

When you are missing television, I want to encourage you to do something different:

- Pick up a book and read.
- Clean out that closet you've been ignoring forever.
- Plant those flowers for springtime beauty.
- Go outside and "play" as you used to when you were a child.
- Take a bike ride or a walk in the neighborhood.
- Read your Bible and talk to God.
- Take a much-needed nap.
- Write in your journal; write your dreams and your hopes and your fears.
- Take another nap.

Remember, this time is for you. Do what brings you joy and what fills you up. The point is that you come back to the place where you can walk with strength, run with perseverance, and fly like the eagles. This is what God promises for you!

There is life beyond the TV. It will surprise you, and it might bring out some of the child in you. You might feel more rested and even ready to take off again. So take this challenge to heart and see what it is like to live life without being TV-trapped.

Questions for Reflection and Discussion

1. How much time do you think you spend watching TV and movies each week?

2. Do you watch TV alone or in a group? How do you experience TV differently when you are alone versus with friends or family?

3. What is the main topic of your TV time? For example, do you watch crime shows, reality TV, game shows, comedies, cooking shows, and so forth?

4. What do you hope to do with your extra time this week without TV?

5. In what ways does your soul need rest? When is the last time you felt energized and fully rested?

6. How can your connection with God improve?

Prayer

Dear God, today I am reminded that I have put the television before you. Forgive me for my idolatry of spending more time with it than with you. Help me to know your love fully again. Give me ears to hear your voice whispering encouragement. Give me space to know joy through the experience of your creation. Give me the ability to walk strong, run well, and to fly to the mountaintops of my life. I need your help, God, for I am weary, and weak, and tired. And I have become trapped. Energize me, for I am forever grateful for your love and mercy. Thank you, God! Amen.

Focus for the Week

Take six days without the television, including without Internet movies you may watch on your computer. In place of the time you would spend watching these shows, do things that provide you with rest and restoration of your soul.

1. From *Rest in the Storm, Self-Care Strategies for Clergy and Other Caregivers*, by Kirk Byron Jones (Judson Press, 2001); pages 7-8.
2. From *Rest in the Storm, Self-Care Strategies for Clergy and Other Caregivers*; page 10.
3. From *Rest in the Storm, Self-Care Strategies for Clergy and Other Caregivers*; page 11.
4. From "Precious Lord, Take My Hand," *The United Methodist Hymnal* (Copyright © 1989 by The United Methodist Publishing House); 474.
5. A variation of the traditional lullaby, "Mockingbird."
6. From "Americans spend 34 hours a week watching TV, according to Nielsen numbers," by David Hinckley for *New York Daily News*, September 19, 2012. *www. nydailynews.com/entertainment/tv-movies/americans-spend-34-hours-week-watching-tv-nielsen-numbers-article-1.1162285*. Accessed March 29, 2014.

Hello? Anyone There?

Scripture: Read Daniel 3:19-27

GIVE IT UP: No cell phones for a week

GAIN: Release from addiction to phones and increase in knowing God's faithfulness

The evolution of our communication system is fascinating. It likely began with storytellers sharing narratives around campfires, narratives that provided instruction, moral guidance, and connection. Then we had horseback delivery of letters. The written word came in personal form and at the personal peril of the rider and the horse. Then mail became the source of information, delivered via trucks and trains. Mail became a key avenue of our communication. I remember writing letters to my grandparents on birthdays and sending letters to my boyfriend when I lived in another state. Newspapers were a main source of information sharing; we read them from front to back, and we talked about the day's events in coffee shops, at work, and on our front porches. There was also the telephone; we could call each other, although it was different from today.

When I was young, we had the old phones that either hung on our wall or sat on an end table. They were usually black and had rotary dial (remember that?). You put your finger into the dial hole above the number needed and rotated the dial around to the end; then you repeated that process for each number. There was a series of clicks and sounds with each spin of the dial. I still love that sound. Someone should make a ringer sound out of that for our smartphones.

For a while, we had a party line. This was a cheaper version of coverage in which you shared a phone line with a number of other families. So you might pick up the phone and find someone from the family down the street talking on it. Sometimes you would hear bits and pieces of conversations not intended for you. I believe the party line did much for the advancement of the rumor mill in town.

We had a long cord on our phone. So when your boyfriend called, you could stretch the cord around the corner and sit on the floor, hoping none of your family members would hear the conversation. Some of our phone cords had been stretched so long and so often that they were permanently misshapen. Sharing a phone in this way meant you could talk on the phone only for a certain period before Mom or Dad would yell, "Get off the phone!" And until you did, your brothers and sisters and parents got to hear bits and pieces of your side of the phone conversation.

If a call was long distance, that meant it was very important (and very costly), and so you would run and notify the person being called. There was an adrenaline rush around a long-distance phone call.

When you were away from your home and you needed to make a call—perhaps because Mom or Dad forgot to pick you up at school—you would have to find a pay phone, put a dime in it, and make your call, and then run back to the place where you were waiting for them to pick you up.

If you were lost, you had to pull out a paper map or stop at a gas station for directions. And if you were late for a gathering, no one knew why you were late until you showed up. If there was an emergency, you just relied on friends or strangers to rescue you.

Because of these old ways of using the phone, direct community connection was strong. The phone was a *supplementary* source of communication; talking to people face to face was the core communication skill.

While I wouldn't want to go back to the "olden days," I sometimes long for the quiet and the freedom from interruption that existed before cell phones. I have even had days when I envisioned throwing my cell phone at the wall so that it wouldn't work for a while. While I have never done that, it shows how deeply the phone has become entrenched in my life. Once my cell phone became a regular part of my life, I never just turned it off or left it behind on purpose. Our cell phones are like another appendage, and we feel naked without them.

Cell Phone Facts

According to Digital Buzz Blog, we have become BFFs (best friends forever) with our cell phones. Listen to these numbers as of the year 2013:

- 91 percent of people have a mobile phone;
- the average age for getting one's first cell phone is 13;

- 80 percent of cell phone users use it while watching TV;
- 80 percent of time on cell phones is spent in apps;
- we use our cell phones 1.8 hours a day on average;
- 44 percent of cell phone users have slept with their phone so they didn't miss a notification;
- it was projected that by December 2013, there would be more mobile devices than people on the earth.[1]

Pew Research also notes some additional facts:

- 67 percent of us check our cell phones for messages, alerts, and calls when the phone is not ringing or vibrating;
- 29 percent of cell phone users say they "can't imagine living without" their cell phone.[2]

I wonder if that last statistic is lower than reality. Our cell phones have become reliable companions, and we use them for communication, information, business, and bills. They are good, powerful tools, but when it comes to actual interaction, they are a lesser means of communication than face-to-face conversation. They are good tools, but they are *not* our best friend.

Sometimes it seems that we are replacing personal, one-on-one communication with the less intimate cell phone. We have even moved away from talking on the phone to texting on the phone. Now, texting is to talking as e-mail is to snail mail.

Don't get me wrong; I am thankful for my cell phone. It lets me work remotely and frees me up to go to pray for people in hospitals, meet people at coffee shops, attend rallies, squirrel away to study, and even get directions while I am away from the office or my home. I can check e-mails, answer short texts, and post on a blog all while away from my computer. I am especially grateful that when my parents were ill, I was able to be with them in hospitals and rehabilitative facilities while still being in touch with work—remotely, of course. I am grateful for my cell phone.

Addicted to Cell Phones

But there is a problem. It's sometimes called *addiction*, or, if you can't handle that word, *overuse* (the softer version of the same idea). We are, myself included, addicted to our cell phones. Author Brad Lamm calls it a "digital addiction."[3] (By the way, I am also addicted to coffee, Apple products—including the iPhone—and authentic Mexican food.) Being addicted to the cell phone brings with it some particular problems.

Psychologists who deal with people who are addicted say you can know if you have an addiction to cell phones the same way you know if you are addicted to anything else. Check out these addiction signs to see if they apply to your cell phone use:

- tolerance—decreased value requiring more use to get the same effect
- withdrawal
- increased use
- inability to cut back on use
- reduction of competing behaviors
- engaging in the behavior despite risks and negative consequences

- keeping your phone nearby
- thinking frequently about your phone
- interrupting activities to respond to your phone
- feeling distressed without your phone[4]

Cell phones exist for social interaction, and the generations of Internet natives are the ones who have to decide what is normal and what is excessive for their time. Together, we can set boundaries for healthy use of any tool, including cell phones.

The Scripture Story

So what do cell phones have to do with Shadrach, Meshach, and Abednego? Let's dig a little and find out.

The first part of the Book of Daniel contains stories about four young men who were captured and taken to Babylon. They were named Daniel, Hananiah, Mishael, and Azariah. In Babylon, the chief official renamed them: Daniel became Belteshazzar; Hananiah became Shadrach; Mishael became Meshach; and Azariah became Abednego (Daniel 1:6-7). These four men—probably teenagers—were from Jerusalem's noble families, and they were chosen to be educated, trained, and prepared for leadership in Babylon. They were sent to a special school. They went to the best conferences on leadership. They were given the best food. They had the ultimate gym membership.

The young men stood up for their beliefs, even while in training. For example, the food they were given was not kosher, so they requested that they be fed only water and

vegetables instead of the rich meals from the king's table. The chief official initially denied this request, but finally he agreed to try it out for ten days. If they could prove they were still strong and healthy after ten days on that diet, he would allow them to eat as they wished. So they ate only vegetables and water for ten days and were stronger and healthier than all the others who ate the rich foods (Daniel 1:8-16).

While they excelled in their training for leadership in the Babylonian empire and in the service of King Nebuchadnezzar, they held fast to their original faith in the one true God, and they refused to worship any other god.

One day, King Nebuchadnezzar had a huge gold statue built. It was ninety feet high and nine feet thick. He set up the statue and ordered all the important leaders to come to the dedication ceremony. For some reason, Daniel wasn't present, but Shadrach, Meshach, and Abednego were there. The ceremony began with an announcement that when the band started playing, everyone had to bow down to the statue, or they would be thrown into a flaming hot furnace (Daniel 3:1-7).

The band began to play and everyone bowed down—except for Shadrach, Meshach, and Abednego. The Babylonian fortunetellers stepped up and tattled on the three young, Jewish men. They told the king that they were ignoring him and his order (Daniel 3:8-12). So Shadrach, Meshach, and Abednego were brought before King Nebuchadnezzar. The king reprimanded them and gave them a second chance to bow before the gold statue. But they told the king, "We don't need to answer your question. If our God—the one we serve—is able to rescue us from the furnace of flaming fire and from your power, Your Majesty, then let him rescue us. But if he doesn't, know this for certain, Your Majesty: we will

never serve your gods or worship the gold statue you've set up" (Daniel 3:16-18).

King Nebuchadnezzar was so furious his face twisted with rage, and he ordered the servants to make the fire seven times hotter, tie up the hands and feet of the three young men, and throw them into the fiery, hot furnace. The king's men stoked up the fire and made it blazing hot, but when they threw Shadrach, Meshach, and Abednego into the fire, the hot flames devoured the men who were throwing them in! (Daniel 3:19-23).

King Nebuchadnezzar was watching, and he noticed that when he looked into fire, there were four men walking around in the flames! The fourth man looked like a god! And Shadrach, Meshach, and Abednego—well, they were unharmed. They were just walking around, like nothing bad was happening! He called out, "Shadrach, Meshach, and Abednego, servants of the Most High God, come out!" (3:26).

And then Shadrach, Meshach, and Abednego walked out of the fire. When they entered the room, not a hair was singed, not a scorch mark was on their clothes, and they didn't even smell like fire!

When I was a senior in high school, our family home burned down on Christmas Day. It was a devastating moment in many ways, but all of my family made it out safely, so I was grateful, to say the least. However, I remember how the smell of ashes remained in my nostrils for weeks. It seemed like every stitch of clothing I had (and only what I had on survived the fire) smelled like smoke. My hair smelled like smoke. My skin smelled like ashes. My nose hairs kept me smelling smoke for weeks. I can't imagine being near a fire without smelling like smoke!

The king was amazed at what he saw, and he made an instant declaration: "May the God of Shadrach, Meshach, and Abednego be praised! He sent his messenger to rescue his servants who trusted him. They ignored the king's order, sacrificing their bodies, because they wouldn't serve or worship any god but their God. I now issue a decree to every people, nation, and language: whoever speaks disrespectfully about Shadrach, Meshach, and Abednego's God will be torn limb from limb and their house made a trash heap, because there is no other god who can rescue like this" (3:28-29).

Despite this declaration, it seems that King Nebuchadnezzar didn't learn a whole lot, as he continued to use violence and oppression as a form of extreme discipline. But he did learn to respect the God whom the three young men worshipped.

The point of this story is that Shadrach, Meshach, and Abednego held fast to worshipping and following their God, and they refused to bow down to the things around them that went against the grain of their faith. They were thrown into a different culture, and even became leaders in that culture, but they held on to the one thing that mattered: obeying God.

Cell Phones and Shadrach, Meshach, and Abednego

Neither the Congress nor the President of the United States has ordered us to bow down to the world of the cell phone. But culture dictates that we have a cell phone to operate and function fully in our present society. So our culture makes the rules, but sometimes we forget to set a few boundaries on what governs us. Shadrach, Meshach, and Abednego were able to figure out which parts of culture they could live with and which wouldn't work in terms of their faith in God.

We, too, can make that same choice. Will we be bound, hands and feet, enslaved to a phone; or will we set some limits on our use of this popular gadget so that we can follow God's instructions for life?

So I'm asking you to set yourself free this week by giving up some of your time on your cell phone. As always, I want you to continue to use this tool at work and in emergencies if needed. But find some time this week when you go without or function differently with your phone. Here are some ideas for how to implement this fast:

- go one, three, or six days without your phone, except for purposes of work or emergency;
- set your phone on silent and turn off the vibrate mode, and only check it a few times a day;
- turn off all the alerts except for the ringer of a call, so that you don't know when you receive Tweets, Facebook responses, e-mails, or game notifications;
- when you get home, set your phone in one part of the house, and do not carry it around with you from room to room;
- text or check your phone only three times a day, perhaps right before you eat your meals.

We are giving up being ruled by our phones so that we can gain what Shadrach, Meshach, and Abednego lived out. Following God means putting God first and setting boundaries on the surrounding culture. Boundaries can help us live lives that are pleasing to God and healthy for us. Our cell phones are not evil, but they can take up so much of our lives that we have little time or thought for the things of God. Because we want to set ourselves apart for connection with God, we don't want to be ruled by or addicted to things that take us away from God. We want to be faithful to God, as God is faithful to us.

So, I invite you to a journey that is cell-phone-lite or maybe even cell-phone-free for a week. You decide. Do whatever seems beneficial for you regarding your cell phone. Look deep, and ask yourself:

- Do I spend too much time on my phone?
- Is my phone a tool for making life better or a distraction that separates me from the people I love—or both?
- How can I limit my use of the cell phone and increase my time talking to people face to face?
- Can I find more time to be with God, instead of my phone, this week?

Taking Care of Mom

When my mother was in the dying process—having strokes, hospitalizations, and heart attacks—I carried my cell phone with me everywhere. It was with me in my car, in the hospitals, at work, and I even took it with me into the bathroom. I would be in a slight panic if I didn't have my phone nearby in case I got a call and needed to get to Mom's room quickly. I was fearful of missing a call. I didn't want to miss being there when Mom needed me.

And so I carried my phone with me everywhere. I had three chargers to keep it working: one in my purse, which I used at the office; one at home; and one in the car. And I answered my phone no matter what meeting I was in.

But after Mom died, it took about a week before I could lay down my phone in one room and go to another room without it. I had to release my dependence on the phone because there was no longer a need to be present 24-7 for an emergency. I had to remind myself that if my children called and I didn't answer, they knew where I lived and could find me. I had to tell myself that work would always be there and that I didn't have to take every call. I had my daughter, Sara, help me turn off my beeps and reminder sounds so that I could let my spirit rest and find calm again. I had to discipline myself to be free from my phone, so that I could be free to follow God in some old and some new ways.

I invite you to this journey of giving something up so that you can be free to follow God. It might be a little uncomfortable, and it might be difficult, but it will likely bring you a peace you've forgotten you could have.

And after you put your phone down, talk to someone face to face, and listen for their feelings as they talk to you. Or take time to see God in the stars and the sunrise, and listen for God's direction in your life.

And like Shadrach, Meshach, and Abednego, find the freedom of walking around in the fire of life, knowing you are free from what binds you, and you are in the presence of the One who rescues you.

Questions for Reflection and Discussion

1. Are you addicted or overly connected to your phone? How do you know?

2. How has cell phone usage become a distraction in your relationships with others? Or how have you kept it from becoming so?

3. Have you spent more time on your phone than with God each week? What changes can you make to be present to God instead of to your phone?

4. Do you get anxious without your phone? Describe what it feels like to be without your phone.

5. What would the world be like today if we did not have cell phones?

6. Where and how does God speak to you?

Prayer

Dear God, please free me from my constant need to be available to others. And help me know that my connection to you matters the most. Have patience with me as I have allowed life's tools to distract me from loving you and loving others as you love them. Calm my soul as I release myself from the grip of my phone. Strengthen me with the peace that passes all gadgets, all other connections, and all culture. Help me, God, to center on you this week. Meet me in the places and the spaces I make for you. Amen.

Focus for the Week

Give up your cell phone use for six days. Use it for work or family emergencies only. But even at work, try to go without it as much as possible. If it is not possible to lay down your phone for six days, do it for three, or even for one. Another option is to set limits or boundaries on your usage, as stated above. As you release your overuse of this tool, you will find God's faithful and steadfast presence in your life.

1. From "Infographic: 2013 Mobile Growth Statistics," by *Digital Buzz Blog*, October 1, 2013. *www.digitalbuzzblog.com/infographic-2013-mobile-growth-statistics/*. Accessed April 5, 2014.

2. From "Mobile Technology Fact Sheet," by *Pew Research Center's Internet Project*, January 2014. *www.pewinternet.org/fact-sheets/mobile-technology-fact-sheet/*. Accessed April 5, 2014.

3. From "Tips to Overcoming Digital Addiction," by Brad Lamm for *The Huffington Post*, May 6, 2013. *http://www.huffingtonpost.com/2013/05/03/overcoming-internet-addiction-from-brad-lamm-marlo-thomas-mondays-with-marlo_n_3210652.html*. Accessed April 5, 2014.

4. From "Are You Addicted to Your Cell Phone?" by Ira Hyman for *Psychology Today*, March 27, 2013. *www.psychologytoday.com/blog/mental-mishaps/201303/are-you-addicted-your-cell-phone*. Accessed April 5, 2014.

Deep Silence

Scripture: Read Matthew 21:1-11 and Matthew 27:45-56

GIVE IT UP: Mirrors, social media, talking, TV and Internet stations, and cell phones

GAIN: The power of living without distraction and the benefit of silence

The First Scripture Story: Matthew 21:1-11

The week started out at full roar. Jesus' preparation for the Passover meal turned into a community event with the obtaining of a donkey for a ride into Jerusalem. It seemed that, for a moment, everyone finally understood *who* Jesus was: the Son of God, the hoped-for Messiah! I can imagine the disciples were ecstatic as they saw the crowd's adoration. People were throwing down their coats as they did for the royal family, and they were waving palm branches to hail the new "King." Probably the disciples saw this acclaim for Jesus as what they worked so hard for, and they likely basked in the reflection of his moment of glory!

Their hardship of leaving all to follow him and their pain of being misunderstood by family and friends was now worth it all. Jesus was front-and-center in the political world, and he would change things for them and for their people. The disciples must have expected they would be a part of that great movement for change.

The crowd was thrilled as well. This wandering "nobody from Nazareth" had been collecting fans and followers everywhere he went. It seemed like he was a wise teacher and a miracle worker extraordinaire, but he lacked focus around religion and politics. He ticked off too many people along the way, and although he had great potential, everyone knew that you couldn't survive politics without a few friends. But now, it seemed, Jesus had learned how to use his power and charisma for good. It appeared that he was finally leaning into the role of "Savior of the world."

So the people, aware of the change in the climate of their lives, pulled out all the stops and made an instant parade, complete with "Hosannas!" and palm branches, and even the laying down of their coats to pave the way for the Savior, Jesus.

You know how it is at a parade. You cheer and applaud and jump up and down with excitement for all the floats and bands and dancers passing by. I remember one parade I went to in Phoenix that included a surprise group of dancers called "The Dancing Grannies." The surprise was that you didn't expect to see women of advanced age dancing down Central Avenue. They were amazing in their skill, stamina, and expressions of pure joy. The crowd went wild when they passed by, and people jumped up and cheered with wild abandon. The feeling was that if *they* could dance, so could we. Parades do that to people. They bring us back to the places where we experience childlike joy and abandon, and where we forget our other lives as corporate bosses, middle managers, or blue-collar workers. They let us forget our differences and just enjoy life.

When the Bottom Fell Out

But the bottom fell out of the disciples' world when Jesus gathered them to share that Passover meal. The hint of things to come was when Jesus told them that one of them would betray him. He pointed out that Judas, the one who kept their books in order, would bring wrongdoing into their close-knit group (Matthew 26:20-25). They couldn't imagine Judas doing that, but Jesus' words must have sent chills down their spines. You never know what people are capable of.

And it only got worse. Jesus prayed that night in deep agony, and sweat of blood dripped down his face. They had never seen him like this, and it was as hard to watch as it was to stay awake during their prayer time at the Garden of Gethsemane (Matthew 26:36-46).

And then the unimaginable happened: Judas turned Jesus in to the authorities, who showed up in the garden and arrested him! (Matthew 26:47-56). Now their world changed. Weren't they just celebrating and praising in the parade? How did life fall apart so quickly?

Jesus was carted away by the soldiers, and the disciples scattered. Some of them hid out, afraid they too would be arrested. Some of them hung close by so they could find out what was going on. And Peter, who at least had the courage to be close by, faltered in fear when a stranger questioned him; he denied that he even knew Jesus. The disciples were now scattered, fearful, and running for their lives. They were, in fact, disciples without a teacher. They didn't know what to do with themselves (Matthew 26:56-75).

The events marched on without pause. Jesus was tried, condemned, paraded through the streets carrying the cross, and finally crucified (Matthew 27:1-44).

The Second Scripture Story: Matthew 27:45-56

How in the world did this change happen so quickly? They went from celebration to devastation in just a few days. And even the cosmos groaned when the skies turned dark for three hours in the middle of the day (verse 45).

Then Jesus, hanging on the cross, yelled out, "My God, my God, why have you left me?" (verse 46).

Jesus cried out in the pain and agony of feeling alone. And the truth of the matter is, we didn't see that coming. We never expected to hear Jesus have the same feeling of abandonment that we sometimes feel. But now, when we cry out to God feeling abandoned and alone, we can remember that Jesus felt the same. In that moment, he felt totally alone.

When he cried out, some viewers nearby thought he was calling for Elijah. They made fun of him, mocking him because, of course, Elijah wouldn't be coming to save him. They gave him a drink of sour wine on a dirty sponge, reminiscent of the sponges we swab patients' mouths with when they are forbidden to drink before a surgery. Jesus' last drink was sour wine on a stick. This was given to the One whose first miracle was turning water into wine, and the guests were amazed that the best wine was saved for last (John 2:1-11). Yet his last drink of wine was so bad it tasted like vinegar.

And then, finally, the agony ended as Jesus cried out one more time and took his last breath. The whole universe responded to the last breath. The curtain in the Temple ripped in two, and the earth quaked so that rocks split. Tombs were disturbed, and some dead people arose from their graves (verses 51-53).

The wide-ranging response was so impressive that those guarding Jesus were terrified. Having mocked Jesus just a few moments before, now they cried out, "This was certainly God's Son" (verse 54).

Some women were there, including Mary Magdalene, Mary the mother of James and Joseph, and the mother of Zebedee's sons. Two mamas and a close friend remained with Jesus until the end, saw his last breath, saw the world groan, and must have hung their heads in sorrow deeper than any they had ever known (verses 55-56).

And then there was silence. After all the hoopla and all the excitement, the fear and the abandonment, there was only silence. It was done. Jesus died. The world cried. The women had nothing to say.

Silence roars when the previous moments are filled with noisy chaos. That makes silence stand out, and it makes silence stretch out over eons of time. Sometimes silence is so noticeable, it thunders.

When Silence Is Our Teacher

Silence implies waiting for something to happen. The absence of noise seems to imply a lack of vitality. But that's not always the message of silence. Sometimes silence is our greatest teacher. If we can lean into the stillness and quiet that is silence, we just might learn our deepest lessons.

The art of meditation is about putting ourselves in a position of nothingness so that we can be filled and so that we can listen and hear differently. When learning how to meditate, you can find a way to let go of thoughts by focusing on your breathing, or by repeating a one- or two-word mantra. If we stay focused, eventually we will move into the place of stillness and silence that brings healing and health and strength.

Arianna Huffington, in her book *Thrive*, tells of a study out of the University of North Carolina, in which professor Barbara L. Fredrickson made the connection between meditation and an increase in positive emotions. Those included "love, joy, gratitude, contentment, hope, pride, interest, amusement," and they resulted in "increases in a variety of personal resources, including mindful attention, self-acceptance, positive relations with others, and good physical health."[1]

Meditation has been a part of spiritual development throughout time, and wise teachers have often utilized it as a way to connect with God through silence. Praying, though often taught as a "conversation" with God, is more connectional when it is also an act of listening. Often our prayers go something like this:

*Dear God, please help me with my [insert problem].
Here's what's going on: And I know this [insert
desired solution] will fix the situation. Please make
[the desired outcome] happen so that I can have a
happy life again. Thank you for hearing me, Lord.
And please hurry up. Amen.*

When we pray like this, we are not only telling God what
we think we need, we are directing God to make the outcome
exactly what we ask. In other words, we are bossing God
around. But if we realize that God knows about our life and
sees our situations differently, then we can take a stance of
humility and say something like this:

*Dear God, I don't know what to do about [insert
problem] anymore. Nothing I've tried has worked.
Please help me see this situation as you see it. And
direct me to follow your way. I'm listening, God.
Please direct me. Amen.*

After a prayer like this, we should take time to sit in silence
and hear God. We may not hear actual words, but we may
receive deep peace and even wisdom. We might receive a new
idea about our life that is out of the ordinary. God may direct
us in surprising ways, if we are willing to listen instead of
directing God.

It takes deep silence to change our lives and to live humbly
before God. The psalmist knew this when he stated, "Be still,
and know that I am God!" (Psalm 46:10, NRSV).

Knowing God requires hearing, and hearing happens best in silence.

Give Up All the Things That Distract Us From God

This week, I am asking you to attempt to give up all of the things you gave up previously—but all at once. So for six days, try to give up mirrors, social media, talking, TV/Internet stations, and cell phones (except for work or emergencies). This is the hardest week, and it will require dedication.

Most of us will not be able to do this completely unless we go on a personal retreat away from our community. But if you try it at home, you will take note of how often your life is interrupted by the distractions. You will become aware of the noise that dampens the ability to hear God's voice.

So I recommend that you try to implement periods of silence every day. Maybe the hour you spend in between work and home is a time when you can shut everything down and just inhabit silence. Or perhaps you can wake up and start your day in silence until you arrive at work. In whatever form you choose to implement it, take note of the distractions, but live in the silence. The hope is that your moments of silence will be powerful enough for you to start a new habit of incorporating silence into your everyday routine.

It is not easy. Just today, while writing this lesson, I was irritated because my Internet connection went down. This affected my TV and my computer. My first reaction was to play music. The need to fill in the space was so great and so strong that I was uncomfortable with silence. The next thing

I did was call the cable company to get it fixed, but the phone lines were busy. So I sat back and laughed at myself for writing about silence while fighting against it, and then I turned off the music and let my fingers talk, without distraction.

It is not easy to be quiet. We might be afraid of what we will hear when we listen. Or we might like our current lives so much that we don't want God to direct us in any new way, and so we turn up the volume. But silence is a great teacher. God lives in the stillness and in the quiet, and it is there that we will find God.

Questions for Reflection and Discussion

1. Were you able to delete all five items from your days this week (mirrors, social media, talking, TV/Internet stations, and cell phones)? If not, share what periods during the week you were able to find deep silence.

2. What did you find was your greatest distraction from hearing God?

3. After being on this journey to give it up for God, are there any habits you'd like to change? What are they?

4. Did you spend any time meditating? Describe the experience and any benefits or difficulties.

5. How did you hear God differently this week?

Prayer

Dear God, I lead such a noisy, busy, rushed life. It's no wonder that I can't always hear you. But I am committing to slowing down and to finding quiet and stillness in the days of this week. Help me as I go on this journey to hear you, to notice my distractions, and to make changes that will affect the rest of my life. I need your help. I don't know how to go through life without you. So, dear God, direct me, hold me, calm me, and bring me closer to your love. I am yours. Amen.

Focus for the Week

Give up mirrors, social media, talking, TV/Internet stations, and cell phones for six days or at least for a designated portion of each day.

1. From *Thrive: The Third Metric to Redefining Success and Creating a Life of Well-Being, Wisdom, and Wonder*, by Arianna Huffington (Harmony Books, 2014); page 45.

The Meet-Up

Scripture: Read Matthew 28:1-10

GIVE IT UP: Give it up in applause and praise for the one who wants to meet up with you and me

GAIN: An encounter with Jesus, the Christ who provides direction for our lives

The Scripture Story

After the Sabbath, as the first light of the new week dawned, Mary Magdalene and the other Mary came to keep vigil at the tomb. Suddenly the earth reeled and rocked under their feet as God's angel came down from heaven and came right to where they were standing. He rolled back the stone and then sat on it. Shafts of lightning blazed from him. His garments shimmered snow-white. The guards at the tomb were scared to death. They were so frightened that they couldn't move.

The angel spoke to the women: "Don't be afraid" (or as *The Message* words it, "There is nothing to fear here"). The angel continued, "I know that you are looking for Jesus who was crucified. He isn't here, because he's been raised from the dead, just as he said. Come, see the place where they laid him. Now hurry, go and tell his disciples, 'He's been raised from the dead. He's going on ahead of you to Galilee. You will see him there.' I've given the message to you" (verses 5-7).

The women, deep in wonder and full of joy, lost no time in leaving the tomb. They ran to tell the disciples. Then Jesus met them and greeted them, stopping them in their tracks. They fell to their knees, embraced his feet, and worshipped him. Jesus said, "You're holding on to me for dear life! Don't be frightened like that. Go tell my brothers that they are to go to Galilee, and that I'll meet them there" (verse 10, *The Message*).

That Familiar Scripture

When I was young, I learned a song that you probably know: "Twinkle, Twinkle Little Star." The lyrics, written in the 1800's by Jane Taylor, were so familiar in my day that everyone could sing it:

Twinkle, twinkle little star,
How I wonder what you are.
Up above the world so high,
Like a diamond in the sky.
Twinkle, twinkle little star,
How I wonder what you are.

Something about that song connects to my childhood. It's so familiar that I can sing it without thinking about it. I know the words by heart. Probably you do too.

The song, however, has its primary meaning for me when I sit outside at night, look at the stars, ponder the amazing beauty of God's world, and wonder how God could do all that. Then I think of the song as a philosophical treatise that expresses our deepest wish to know how things work and who God is. That is when the song touches me deeply.

This week's Scripture story is like the song "Twinkle, Twinkle Little Star." If we grew up in church, the story is so familiar that it can be heard as a backdrop to our lives but without deep impact. Even if we attend church on Christmas and Easter only, this is one story we really do know about our faith, because we hear it every other time we go to church each year. So as with all things familiar, its meaning can fade if we don't pay attention.

But today, I hope we can sit up and take note of what God is saying to us in the Easter story and in the Resurrection event.

Recent Meet-Up With Josie, My Almost-Daughter

I recently met up with my almost-daughter Josie. She's a woman with a family and a full life in another state, but I had lost contact with her for most of her growing up years, and it was a wonderful surprise to find her again.

I met her when she was just a toddler. Her mother, Elly, came to the mission in Nogales, where I grew up, and became a resident for a time while she was getting her feet back under her. Josie, her daughter, was there with her. Josie had dark brown hair, beautiful brown skin, and a smile that lit up the world. She loved people—all people—and we bonded pretty quickly. I was a teenager and really enjoyed any time I had with Josie. We were so connected that one time Elly asked me if I would raise Josie if anything were to happen to her. I said, "Of course!" without even thinking. I adored this little, brown-eyed bundle of love!

I went off to college, and Elly and Josie moved on to Tucson. The first year I was gone, I got a devastating call from my mom. She informed me that Elly died while sky diving out of a plane. Her parachute didn't open, and she fell to her death. My first question to my mom was if I could raise Josie. I was already figuring out the logistics of raising Josie while I went to college.

Mom informed me that Josie had an uncle and aunt in Michigan, and they would now parent her. I understood that she needed to be with family, and I was just a college student; but in my heart, I felt like she was really my daughter. And I grieved that I wouldn't be her replacement mom.

I lost track of Josie, but thanks to the miracle of Facebook, we connected again. Josie met me when I went to Michigan, and then she brought her family to Arizona for a vacation. We met at a restaurant, and as I sat with her family of three beautiful daughters and a loving husband, it occurred to me that God had taken good care of Josie in placing her with her aunt and uncle. I also had this overwhelming emotion and connection for my almost-daughter, feeling the unearned pride of a mother who sees her child grow up to be happy, healthy, and successful. I went home that day feeling as if a puzzle piece of my life had been put in its right place, and I was grateful for the way God connected us.

Josie and her family then went down to Nogales and visited her mother's grave. Having someone come full circle in our lives is a significant thing, and it can settle us into the sure knowledge of God's love. God heals us and fills us through our meet-ups.

Jesus' Meet-Up

This Gospel story starts with Mary Magdalene and the other Mary approaching the tomb to do their duty and attend to their grief. It was the first light of dawn in the new week. They were expecting only to see a grave and to release their tears, but what they experienced was world-changing for them.

The angel sent them on their way to deliver the message of Jesus' resurrection, and they didn't even stop to check the empty tomb one more time to make sure. They were very sure about what they were experiencing! The Scripture says they left the tomb with "great fear and excitement" (verse 8), and we can understand both emotions. But consider that excitement. Have you ever been deep in wonder and full of joy? Have you had an event happen to you that was so life sustaining that it captivated your sense of wonder and joy?

That happens when a baby is born. I recall the first meet-ups with all four of my children. Even though circumstances varied from a child who would die to a child we adopted to children from healthy births, each meet-up moment was deep in wonder and full of joy! I remember the tears of unexpected joy and the sense of wonder that we were somehow involved in this miracle before us. Perhaps you've had an experience like this.

The Scripture says that as the women hurried from the tomb, Jesus greeted them. Now there is "good morning," and there is "good morning!" When you run into Jesus, the one you saw buried, and the one you were grieving about just seconds before; that "good morning!" will never be forgotten. That "good morning!" turned their lives around. That "good morning!" brought them to their knees, worshipping him and holding on to his ankles as if to keep him from ever leaving them again.

Can you even begin to imagine that moment? It would be like Josie meeting her mother who had died! It would be amazing like that!

Jesus reassured them and told them not to be afraid. Then he sent them on, instructing them to go Galilee, where they would meet up and talk more.

The Greatest Miracle

There are miracles in this story that make us stop and ponder. There is the angel who appears in bright, brilliant light. Angels are not part of our ordinary experience, so when we think of one appearing to us, the word *miracle* comes to mind. But the angel was not the greatest miracle in this story.

There is the empty grave. If you buried your son or your best friend, and you went to the grave the next day to release your tears but found it empty, you might think that was a miracle. Such was the case for the two Marys. They went to the grave-cave and watched the angel roll the stone away. They accepted the invitation to look in and see the empty space where Jesus' body had been. That miracle moment took their breath away. It was a great miracle, but it wasn't the greatest miracle in this story.

Usually when we come to Easter, we think of Resurrection. Because we can't wrap our minds around it, we get stuck in the whole idea of resurrection. We pause there, and we stop and stare and get lost in this concept. But there is more to this story than the resurrected body of Jesus Christ. The Resurrection is surely a miracle that leaves us in open-mouthed wonder, but it is not the whole miracle. It is not even the whole story.

There's another miracle that we rarely notice. It is the miracle of the meet-up! Did you notice in the story what Jesus was doing after he rose from the dead? He was meeting up with Mary and Mary, and he was preparing for the meet-up with the disciples. Later on, he met up with many others (1 Corinthians 15:4-8). His main purpose seemed to be to meet with his friends and give them instructions and last words for the rest of their lives.

Now that is the real miracle! Jesus' concern was for *them*, for connecting with them, for engaging deeply with them, for directing them about their purpose and life in the future. He made it a point to spend the time he had left on the earth connecting with those whom he loved.

Jesus wants a meet-up with you too! Jesus sees your struggles, and hears your questions, and feels your deepest longings, and wants to meet-up with you. He wants to lighten your load, answer your confusion, and fill you with joy. Jesus wants to meet with you, and that is the greatest miracle!

Easter Is Not . . . Easter Is!

So it's important to sort through our understanding of Easter and to know what it is not:

- Easter is *not* the Easter bunny.
- Easter is *not* dyed eggs and yellow Peeps chickens.
- Easter is *not* yummy chocolate, hollow bunnies.
- Easter is *not* bonnets and new dresses.
- Easter is *not* even the family dinner with honey-baked ham and mashed potatoes.

Easter *is* the meet-up between you and Jesus. It is the chance to hear instructions for the rest of your life, to know you are loved and that you matter to God. Easter *is* the connection between you and God.

So stop and listen to the miracle of Easter. It's personal. It's about you knowing God wants to be with you. It's about knowing you are not ever alone and that God will direct you. Don't ever give up, because this is the greatest news of all!

He is risen! He is risen indeed! Enjoy your meet-up with Jesus today!

Questions for Reflection and Discussion

1. In what ways does the Easter story serve as a backdrop in your life?

2. Describe a significant meet-up you have had in your life. What was your main emotion as you encountered that person?

3. Do you get stuck in the idea of resurrection? How do you explain this miracle to yourself?

4. If Jesus called for a meet-up with you, what would you want to ask him?

5. How does the miracle of the meet-up inform your life, change your life, or transform your life?

6. What is the greatest miracle of Easter to you?

Prayer

Risen Savior, forgive us for pausing so long in the miracle of Resurrection that we forget to notice the miracle of your presence in our lives. Help us today to celebrate all that you are in our lives. Help us to embrace your embodiment in our world. Help us to see you in the day-to-day, ordinary moments. Thank you for loving us enough to request a meet-up. Thank you for your direction for our future. Help us to be present for our world as you have been present for us. Amen.

Focus for the Week

This week we include back into our lives all those things we gave up. And we include praise as a special offering, giving it up for God's goodness to us. Remember to be grateful, thankful, and overflowing with praise for Jesus, the one who died, who rose-again, and who invites us to a meet-up!